Fun Fan Facts:

The Unofficial NBA Edition

Atlanta Hawks

Everything Young Hawks Fans Should Know

By: Jake Liam

Dedication

For every Hawks fan who watched Dominique fly,
argued about the Luka trade, and stayed loud anyway.

Atlanta always knew. The rest of the world is just
catching up.

THE NBA BY THE NUMBERS

MOST NBA CHAMPIONSHIPS*

- CELTICS (18) †
- LAKERS (17)
- WARRIORS (7)
- BULLS (6)
- SPURS (5)

As of the 2024-25 Season. † One Trophy = 4 Championships.

BIG NUMBERS

$156 million
Stephen Curry's est. earnings in the 24-25 season

7'7"
Tallest player in NBA history (Gheorghe Mureșan & Manute Bol)

NBA HISTORY SNAPSHOT

- **1946** NBA Founded
- **1954** Shot Clock Introduced
- **1979** 3-Point Line Added
- **2023** NBA Cup Introduced

30 | 4 | 82

- **30** Teams Competing in the NBA
- **4** Playoff Rounds
- **82** Games Per Season

ATLANTA HAWKS
IN THE NBA

- **FOUNDED: 1946** †
- **NBA TITLES: 1**
- **CONFERENCE TITLES: 4** *

10 Consecutive Playoff Appearances (2008–2017)

*† Founding dates are complicated & may cause arguments at Thanksgiving. Ask someone born before color TV. All Titles reflect pre-relocation franchise history. * As of 2024-25 Season.*

EASTERN CONFERENCE

- Atlantic – **Celtics**
- Atlantic – **Nets**
- Atlantic – **Knicks**
- Atlantic – **76ers**
- Atlantic – **Raptors**
- Central – **Bulls**
- Central – **Cavaliers**
- Central – **Pistons**
- Central – **Pacers**
- Central – **Bucks**
- Southeast – **Hawks**
- Southeast – **Hornets**
- Southeast – **Heat**
- Southeast – **Magic**
- Southeast – **Wizards**

WESTERN CONFERENCE

- Pacific – **Lakers**
- Pacific – **Clippers**
- Pacific – **Warriors**
- Pacific – **Suns**
- Pacific – **Kings**
- Northwest – **Nuggets**
- Northwest – **Timberwolves**
- Northwest – **Thunder**
- Northwest – **Trail Blazers**
- Northwest – **Jazz**
- Southwest – **Mavericks**
- Southwest – **Rockets**
- Southwest – **Spurs**
- Southwest – **Pelicans**
- Southwest – **Grizzlies**

NBA ALL-TIME MVP LEADERS

KAREEM ABDUL-JABBAR (6) ★ MICHAEL JORDAN (5) ★ BILL RUSSELL (5)

Introduction

Welcome, fans! Whether you're new to cheering for the Atlanta Hawks or you've been bleeding the team colors your whole life, this book is packed with fun, exciting facts about your favorite team. Get ready to impress your friends and family with everything you know about the Hawks.

Quick Timeout

This book is packed with stats. Like, A LOT of stats. Every fact was checked, double-checked, and triple-checked. But here's the thing about basketball history: not everyone agrees on everything. Ask someone who watched games before color TV and someone who grew up with instant replay and you'll get two completely different answers. My dad, stepdad, uncle, and grandpa all argued about the same fact. Four people. Four answers. All of them think they're right. So if you spot something that doesn't match what you've heard, congratulations. You might be a bigger fan than the people who helped make this book. And honestly? That's pretty cool.

HOW IT WORKS

THE SEASON
82 Games. One Goal.
Each team plays 82 games.
Win enough to make the
Playoffs.
Every game counts!

PLAYOFFS
30 Teams. 16 Make It.
8 per conference make the playoffs.
Win=Advance | Lose=Go Home
Best record
gets home court!

PLAYOFF ROUNDS
Best of 7. Win 4 or Go Home.
4 rounds of pure pressure.
Every series is do-or-die!

OVERTIME?
5 More Minutes.
Keep playing until
someone pulls ahead.
No ties. Ever.

THE FINALS
One Series. One Champion.
Winner lifts the Trophy.
Legend status unlocked.

How the NBA Works

At first glance, basketball feels simple. Ten players. One ball. Two hoops. Go.

Then the NBA adds the layers.

An 82-game regular season. A draft where bad teams pick first. Playoffs that last two full months. Superstars who can change everything with one trade. Dynasties that rise, fall, and rise again.

And somehow, it all works.

The NBA is built on one big idea: every team gets a chance to reset, reload, and rise again. No relegation. No dropping down to a lower league. Just basketball, every night, from October through June.

It is a league designed for drama, stars, and comebacks. And once you understand the flow, it is impossible to stop watching.

The League Setup

The NBA has 30 teams, spread across the United States and Canada. Those teams are split into two conferences:

- Eastern Conference
- Western Conference

Each conference has three divisions, mostly based on geography. Divisions matter for scheduling, but not as much as they used to.

Every team plays 82 regular season games, usually from October through April. Home games. Road games. Back-to-back nights. Long road trips. The season is a marathon before the sprint even starts.

Win games, and you climb the standings. Lose too many, and the pressure builds fast.

How Games Are Played

An NBA game has four quarters, each lasting 12 minutes. That means 48 minutes of game time, plus timeouts, free throws, and the occasional coach argument that adds another 20 minutes nobody planned for.

Scoring is simple:

- A shot inside the three-point line is worth 2 points
- A shot beyond the arc is worth 3 points
- Free throws are worth 1 point

If the score is tied at the end of regulation, the game goes to overtime, which lasts 5 minutes. Still tied? Another overtime. Keep going until someone wins.

There is a shot clock too. Teams have 24 seconds to take a shot. No standing around. No holding the ball forever. Keep it moving.

The Regular Season Race

The regular season is long for a reason. It tests everything.

Depth. Health. Focus. Patience.

Teams play opponents from both conferences, but they face conference rivals more often. By the end of the season, each conference's top teams have earned their playoff spots the hard way.

The goal is simple: make the playoffs. But there is a twist.

The NBA Cup

In 2023, the NBA added something new to the middle of the season. Something with actual stakes. They called it the In-Season Tournament, now known as the NBA Cup.

It works like this: Every team plays a small group stage during November and December, with special court designs that look like nothing else in basketball. The best teams advance to a knockout round held in Las Vegas.

The winners split a prize pool. Players earn bonus money. And for the first time, a team could lift a trophy before the playoffs even started.

Some fans are still warming up to it. Some players love it. But the moment a team starts treating it seriously and a crowd shows up buzzing in December, it feels like something.

Which, honestly, sounds about right.

The Play-In Tournament

Instead of sending the top eight teams from each conference straight to the playoffs, the NBA added something new. The Play-In Tournament.

Here is how it works:

- Teams ranked 1 through 6 in each conference are safe
- Teams ranked 7 through 10 fight for the final two playoff spots

The 7 and 8 seeds have an advantage. Win once and you are in. Lose and you still get one more shot. The 9 and 10 seeds have to win twice in a row just to earn a first-round matchup.

It turns the end of the season into a sprint. Every game suddenly matters more. Fans love it. Coaches age rapidly.

The NBA Playoffs

Once the playoffs begin, everything tightens.

Sixteen teams enter. Eight from each conference. Every round is a best-of-seven games series. That means the first team to win four games moves on:

- First Round
- Conference Semifinals
- Conference Finals
- NBA Finals

Home-court advantage matters. Crowds get louder. Rotations get shorter. Superstars play heavier minutes. One bad quarter can flip a series. One great performance can define a career.

By the time the NBA Finals arrive in June, only two teams are left. One from the East. One from the West. Four wins away from a championship. Four wins away from history.

The NBA Draft: Hope Begins Here

Here is where the NBA gets clever. Every summer, new players enter the league through the NBA Draft. Teams take turns selecting college players, international stars, and teenagers straight out of high school.

The teams that finished with the worst records get the best odds to pick early through the Draft Lottery. It is not guaranteed, but it gives struggling franchises a real shot at changing their future with one pick.

That means one bad season does not doom you forever. It might actually change everything. Some franchises are rebuilt by a single draft night moment.

Hope shows up wearing a new jersey.

No Relegation. All Pressure.

Unlike many global sports leagues, NBA teams never drop down to a lower league. They always stay in the NBA.

That does not mean there is no pressure.

Fans remember losing seasons. Owners make changes. Coaches get replaced. Players get traded. Every year is a test of direction, patience, and belief.

Stars, Systems, and Showtime

The NBA is famous for its stars. But stars do not win alone.

Teams need chemistry. Coaches need systems. Role players need to deliver on the biggest stages. One injury. One hot streak. One trade deadline deal. Any of it can flip a season.

That balance between individual brilliance and team basketball is what makes the league special.

Fast breaks. Buzzer-beaters. Game 7s. And moments that get replayed forever. That is the NBA.

Once you get the flow, it is pure electricity.

Atlanta Hawks Facts

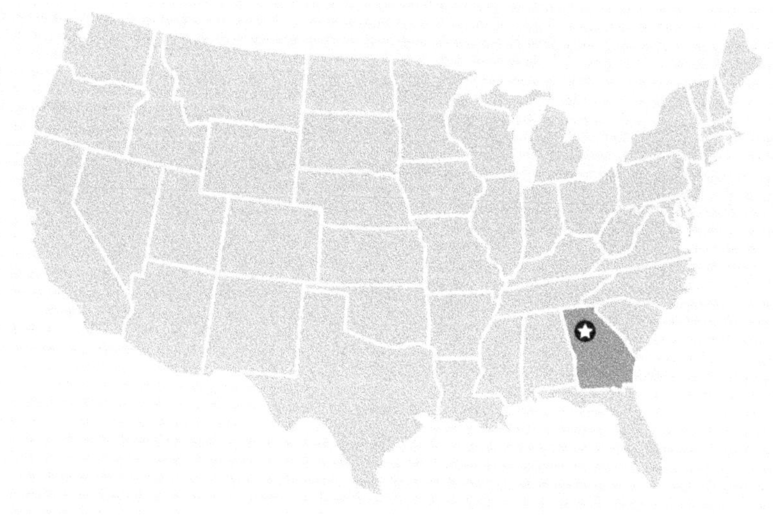

Home City

Atlanta, Georgia

Metro Area Population

About 6.2 Million

Home Arena

State Farm Arena

Arena Capacity

18,118

Conference / Division

Eastern Conference / Southeast Division

Famous Local Food

Peach cobbler, fried chicken, biscuits, sweet tea

Chapter 1: From Tri-Cities to Treetop Town

1. Three Cities, One Very Confused Team

Picture a professional basketball team so restless it couldn't stay in one place long enough to unpack the trophy case. The Atlanta Hawks didn't start in Atlanta. They didn't even start in one city. They started in three of them at the same time, which is either bold vision or a logistical nightmare depending on how you look at it.

In 1946, a franchise called the Tri-Cities Blackhawks launched out of the Quad Cities region straddling Illinois and Iowa. Moline, Rock Island, and Davenport shared one team like three roommates splitting a Netflix password. Nobody was fully satisfied, but everybody got to watch. The "Blackhawks" name honored the legendary Native American leader Black Hawk, who had deep historical ties to the region. The basketball was less legendary. The team flopped around the early NBA like a fish that had taken a wrong turn, searching for footing in a league still figuring out what it wanted to be.

Nobody in Moline looked at that situation and said "yes, this will become the pride of Atlanta someday." But every great road trip starts somewhere weird.

2. Milwaukee, St. Louis, and a Team That Couldn't Sit Still

After Tri-Cities, the Hawks packed up and moved to Milwaukee in 1951. Milwaukee lasted two seasons before the Hawks moved again because apparently Milwaukee was not the answer. Then came St. Louis in 1955, and that is where things finally clicked.

The St. Louis Hawks became a legitimate NBA powerhouse. They won the 1958 NBA Championship, built a passionate fanbase, and had Bob Pettit doing things on a basketball court that made crowds forget what city they were even in. More on Pettit in Chapter 2, and more on that 1958 title in Chapter 3. For a moment it looked like St. Louis had its basketball identity locked in for good.

Then the Hawks moved again anyway. By 1968, shifting demographics, a softening local market, and the gravitational pull of the growing American South had ownership pointing the moving trucks toward Georgia. Atlanta was booming, hungry for major league sports, and ready to say yes to basically anything wearing a jersey. The Hawks arrived and, remarkably, stayed. Three cities. Two false starts. One home. Atlanta had no idea what was walking through the door.

3. Dropping "Black" and Keeping the Swagger

When the team landed in Atlanta, the name was already simply the Hawks. The 'Blackhawks' nickname had been shortened to 'Hawks' back in 1951 when the franchise moved to Milwaukee. Atlanta in the late 1960s was a city in full motion, politically significant, culturally electric, and very much announcing itself to the rest of the country. A sharp one-word name suited that energy considerably better than a hyphenated Midwestern geography lesson.

It turned out to be a perfect edit. Atlanta in the late 1960s was a city in full motion, politically significant, culturally electric, and very much announcing itself to the rest of the country. A sharp one-word name suited that energy considerably better than a hyphenated Midwestern geography lesson. The hawk itself is a fast, precise aerial predator. As Atlanta mascots go, it holds up much better than, say, the Tri-Cities Prairie Dogs would have.

The visual identity shifted over the decades through uniforms, logos, and color schemes that ranged from great to genuinely questionable. But the name never wavered. Sometimes the best rebrand is just knowing what to cut.

4. Atlanta Gets the Call

The Hawks were not Atlanta's first attempt at professional basketball, but they were the one that stuck around long enough to matter. When the team arrived in 1968, Atlanta was already positioning itself as the capital of the New South, a city with major league ambitions and a sports identity still being written from scratch.

The NBA was actively looking to plant flags beyond its northeastern and Midwestern strongholds, and Atlanta was exactly the kind of fast-growing Sun Belt city the league wanted on its map. The Hawks initially played at Alexander Memorial Coliseum on the Georgia Tech campus before moving into bigger venues as the audience grew. It was not an overnight romance. Building a basketball culture inside a football-obsessed region takes time, patience, and at least one player so exciting that people will show up just to see what happens next.

Atlanta is a city that rewards patience with full commitment. Once the right players arrived and gave people a reason to care, the relationship between the Hawks and their city started developing into something worth talking about.

5. State Farm Arena: The House That Keeps Getting Better

The Hawks have lived in several buildings since arriving in Atlanta, but their current home is one of the best arenas in the NBA, and that was not always the case. State Farm Arena opened in 1999 as Philips Arena and spent its early years as a perfectly serviceable venue with all the atmosphere of a large, expensive waiting room.

Then came the renovation. Completed in 2018, the overhaul cost around $192 million and transformed the building into a legitimate modern showpiece. New seating put fans closer to the court. The technology got a full upgrade. The food improved dramatically, which matters more than people admit. The whole thing was funded entirely by the team rather than Atlanta taxpayers, which earned the Hawks considerable goodwill from a city that has seen enough publicly funded stadium debates to last a lifetime.

Sitting in the heart of downtown Atlanta near Mercedes-Benz Stadium, State Farm Arena is now central to one of the busiest sports and entertainment corridors in the South. On the right night, with the crowd fully locked in and Trae Young doing something that should not be physically possible, the place is loud and alive in a way that makes you understand exactly why Atlanta fell for this team.

6. Bob Pettit: The First Great Hawk (1954-1965)

Before the Hawks were Atlanta's team, before the dunks and the finger wags and the deep threes, there was a quiet, methodical forward from Baton Rouge who became the best player in the NBA and made everyone take the franchise seriously for the first time. Bob Pettit was not flashy. He was simply unstoppable.

Pettit became the first player in NBA history to score 20,000 career points, a milestone that sounds routine now and was genuinely earth-shattering then. He won two league MVP awards, made eleven All-Star teams, and led the Hawks to their only NBA championship in 1958. More on that championship in Chapter 3, because it deserves its own spotlight. What belongs here is the picture of a player who was told early in his career that he was too small and too slow to make it in professional basketball, then spent a decade making everyone who said that feel very embarrassed.

Pettit was the kind of player who made coaches look smart just by being on the floor. When the Hawks retired his number 9, it was the first jersey retirement in franchise history. He set the standard for what a Hawk could be, and every great player who came after him walked through a door he built.

Bob Pettit holds the MVP trophy after the 1958 NBA All-Star Game while representing the St. Louis Hawks. The same franchise would later move south and become today's Atlanta Hawks. *Photo: Bob Pettit, 1958 NBA All-Star Game MVP. Public domain. Source: Wikimedia Commons.*

7. Pete Maravich: Pistol Pete (1970-1974)

There are players who are good at basketball, and then there are players who appear to have been designed by someone who found regular basketball a little too boring. Pete Maravich was firmly in the second category. He arrived in Atlanta in 1970 as the most hyped rookie in the league, fresh off a college career at LSU where he averaged over 44 points per game without a three-point line, which feels like something that should not be legal.

His four seasons with the Hawks were electric and complicated in equal measure. The offense ran through him in ways that were thrilling to watch and occasionally maddening to coach. He could do things with a basketball that left opponents standing still simply because their brains needed an extra second to process what had just happened. Behind-the-back passes in traffic. Dribbling combinations that looked more like performance art than basketball. A shooting touch that made difficult shots look like layups.

The Hawks eventually traded him to New Orleans in 1974, a move that disappointed Atlanta fans significantly. Maravich's time in the city was brief but impossible to forget. Some players leave a franchise after four years and barely register. Pistol Pete left after four years and people are still talking about it.

8. Dominique Wilkins: The Human Highlight Film (1982-1994, 1996-1997)

If you need to explain to someone why the Atlanta Hawks matter, you start here. Dominique Wilkins arrived in 1982 via a trade from Utah before he had played a single regular season NBA game, and within a few years he had become the most exciting player on the planet. The nickname said everything. Every time he touched the ball near the basket, something was about to happen that you would want to describe to people later.

Wilkins finished his Hawks career as the franchise's all-time leading scorer, averaging close to 26 points per game across more than a decade in Atlanta. He won the NBA Slam Dunk Contest in 1985 and 1990, putting on performances that players still reference today when talking about the history of that competition. He was a nine-time All-Star, a player who could score from anywhere on the court and make it look like he was not trying particularly hard.

The specific moments that made him a legend, including one unforgettable January night and a playoff duel that still gets replayed every few years, are waiting for you in Chapter 3. What belongs in this chapter is the full picture: a player who gave Atlanta over a decade of basketball that the city did not deserve to see that good that early, and who remains the measuring stick against which every Hawks star gets compared.

9. Dikembe Mutombo: The Finger Wag (1996-2001)

Dikembe Mutombo arrived in Atlanta in 1996 as a free agent from Denver, signed a contract that was enormous for its era, and proceeded to do something Hawks fans had never quite seen before. He made the other team scared to come anywhere near the basket. Not cautious. Not hesitant. Scared.

Mutombo grew up in Kinshasa in the Democratic Republic of Congo and came to the United States on an academic scholarship before Georgetown basketball coach John Thompson noticed that the seven-foot-two pre-med student might have another calling. He became one of the greatest defensive players in NBA history, winning four Defensive Player of the Year awards across his career. His time in Atlanta produced two of those awards and some of the most entertaining blocked shot celebrations the league has ever seen.

The finger wag was the thing. It was the basketball equivalent of your mom's "the look." You saw it coming, you knew you deserved it, and it still got you every single time. After blocking a shot, Mutombo would raise his finger and shake it slowly back and forth, a universal signal meaning something like "not today, not in this building, not against me." It became one of the most iconic gestures in sports, showing up in video games, commercials, and impressions at basketball courts around the world. He was funny, warm, and beloved in Atlanta, a player who gave the city a defensive identity it had never had before. Also, nobody has ever made blocking a shot look quite that theatrical since.

10. Trae Young: Ice Trae (2018-present)

The trade that brought Trae Young to Atlanta looked, on draft night in 2018, like it might be a mistake. The Hawks sent the fifth pick and a future first-round selection to Dallas in exchange for the third pick, which they used to select Young out of Oklahoma. Dallas took a young European player named Luka Doncic with that fifth pick. The internet had opinions immediately.

Young came in small, flashy, and confident in a way that occasionally read as reckless. He could not defend consistently as a rookie. He turned the ball over in spectacular fashion on nights when the offense was not flowing. Atlanta fans had seen enough promising young guards to know that promise does not always convert into production. Then Trae Young started converting.

By his second season he was one of the most dangerous offensive players in the league, averaging 29 points and nearly ten assists per game. The deep pull-up three, launched from several feet beyond the arc with no hesitation whatsoever, became his calling card. The nickname Ice Trae arrived because of his habit of performing best when the moment was largest, an attribute he demonstrated in unmistakable fashion during the 2021 playoffs in a building that was definitely not rooting for him. More on that in Chapter 3.

Chapter 3: The Moments That Made History

11. The 1958 NBA Championship

For a franchise that has moved three times and spent decades as a reliable bridesmaid in the Eastern Conference, the 1958 NBA Championship sits at the center of everything. It is the banner. The one. The proof that the Hawks once stood at the top of the basketball world and nobody could take them down.

The opponent was the Boston Celtics, who were in the middle of building a dynasty so complete it would eventually win eleven titles in thirteen years. The Hawks beat them anyway. The series went six games, with St. Louis winning the final three after falling behind. Game 6 belonged entirely to Bob Pettit, who scored 50 points to close out the championship in a decisive game, in 1958, against the best team in basketball. It was like acing a final exam that the entire class failed, finishing early, and then spending the last ten minutes helping everyone else with theirs. The Celtics went home. The Hawks had their trophy. Pettit had scored half a hundred points in the biggest game of his life and made it look like a completely reasonable thing to do.

The Celtics won the title back the following year and proceeded to win it seven more times in a row after that, which is its own kind of absurd. But 1958 belongs to the Hawks. One championship in franchise history, delivered by one of the greatest individual performances in Finals history. No asterisks. No caveats. Just Bob Pettit and the best night of his career.

12. The Duel: Dominique and Bird Go to War (1988)

On May 22, 1988, the Atlanta Hawks and Boston Celtics played a playoff game that had no business being that good. It was Game 7 of the Eastern Conference semifinals. The stakes were everything. And two of the greatest scorers of their generation decided to treat it like a personal competition to see who could break the other's spirit first.

Dominique Wilkins scored 47 points. Larry Bird scored 34 points total, including 20 in the fourth quarter alone and both players were hitting shots from everywhere on the floor, taking turns answering each other's baskets in the fourth quarter like a conversation conducted entirely in highlight reels. The Boston Garden crowd, not exactly known for applauding opposing players, started acknowledging what Wilkins was doing because there was no other honest response.

Boston won the game 118-116, which still stings Atlanta fans who know the full story of what Wilkins put up that night. But the loss did nothing to diminish what happened. Sports has produced very few individual scoring exhibitions under that kind of pressure, against that quality of opponent, with that much on the line. Wilkins walked off the floor having lost a playoff series and still somehow added to his legend. That is a rare kind of greatness.

13. Dominique's 57-Point Explosion

If the Bird duel showed what Dominique Wilkins could do in the fire of a playoff elimination game, the night of December 10, 1986 showed what he could do when he simply decided it was time to score and no one on the opposing team could do anything meaningful about it.

Wilkins scored 57 points against the Chicago Bulls in a regular season game that turned into a one-man demonstration of offensive basketball (and a classic duel with Michael Jordan). The number stood as the Hawks' single-game scoring record for decades and remains one of the highest-scoring individual performances in franchise history. He hit shots from the post, from the perimeter, off the dribble, and through contact, cycling through essentially every scoring method available to a human being in a basketball uniform.

What made Wilkins remarkable was not just the ceiling but the consistency around it. He was not a player who erupted for 57 one night and then disappeared into ordinary production for weeks. He averaged over 26 points per game for his Hawks career, which means those 57 were the sharp peak of a mountain that was already extremely tall. The Nets went home having witnessed something. Their defensive game plan did not survive contact with the evening.

14. The Season Nobody Saw Coming (2014-15)

In the 2014-15 NBA season, the Atlanta Hawks won 60 games. Sixty. The franchise had never done that before. Most people outside Atlanta did not see it coming, and a fair number of people inside Atlanta were also surprised.

The team that pulled it off had no player averaging over 19 points per game. There was no superstar carrying everyone else to victories while exhausted. There was a

beautifully constructed, deeply balanced roster playing
some of the most fluid team basketball in the league,
led by point guard Jeff Teague, wing players Al Horford
and Paul Millsap, and a supporting cast that understood
their roles with unusual precision. Coach Mike
Budenholzer had built something that looked less like a
typical NBA team and more like a very well-run
machine.

The Hawks finished with the best record in the Eastern
Conference. They earned the number one seed in the
playoffs. They were, by every measurable standard, the
best team in the East that season. They lost to
Cleveland in the conference finals in four games, which
is a genuinely deflating postscript, but the regular
season remains a marker for what Atlanta basketball
can look like when everything is working. The city
noticed. The league noticed. The blueprint was there
for anyone paying attention.

15. Trae Young Silences the Garden (2021)

Madison Square Garden has a way of convincing visitors
that New York is the center of the basketball universe
and everyone else is just visiting. Trae Young decided to
use that energy rather than fight it.

In the first round of the 2021 NBA Playoffs, the Hawks faced the New York Knicks in a series that the Garden crowd treated as a personal matter from the opening tip. They booed Young every time he touched the ball. They cheered his turnovers. They created the kind of hostile environment that either breaks a young player or transforms them into something else entirely. Young chose transformation.

He averaged 29.2 points and 9.5 assists across the series, made the decisive plays in multiple close games, and clinched the series at Madison Square Garden with a dominant 36-point, 9-assist performance in Game 5. He pointed to his wrist after big moments throughout the series, a gesture that needed no explanation. The Hawks won the series, then beat the Milwaukee Bucks to reach the Eastern Conference Finals, the deepest playoff run Atlanta had made in years. Young walked out of New York having turned an entire arena's hostility into fuel and used it to write one of the better individual playoff chapters in recent Hawks history.

Chapter 4: Mascots, Traditions, and Genuinely Weird Stuff

16. Harry the Hawk: The Best Entertainer in the Building

Every NBA team has a mascot. Very few NBA mascots have a reputation. Harry the Hawk has a reputation.

Harry has been the Hawks' official mascot since 1995 and has built a career out of being the most unpredictable entity in State Farm Arena on any given night. He has rappelled from the rafters. He has staged elaborate pregame skits. He has appeared in costumes so committed and random that Hawks fans have come to treat his entrances as their own separate form of entertainment, independent of whatever is happening on the court. He is, by most accounts, one of the most creative and athletic mascots in the entire league. This is a compliment that sounds like a small thing until you try to do what Harry does while wearing a giant foam bird head.

Harry's real talent is reading the room. A good mascot pumps up a crowd when the team is winning. A great mascot keeps the crowd entertained when the team is down fifteen at halftime. Atlanta has had plenty of halftimes where they were down fifteen, which means Harry has had a lot of practice. He has not wasted it.

17. Atlanta, Hip-Hop, and the Loudest Arena in the South

There is a reason visiting players have described walking into State Farm Arena on a loud night as one of the more disorienting experiences in the league. Atlanta is not a city that watches basketball quietly.

The Hawks play in a city that produced OutKast, Lil Jon, Ludacris, Migos, 21 Savage, and a music scene so influential it rewired what popular music sounded like for a solid twenty years. That energy finds its way into the building. The game-day soundtrack at a Hawks game has always run closer to a concert than a sports broadcast, and the organization has leaned into that identity rather than fighting it. Atlanta fans do not politely applaud good plays. They respond to good plays the way the city responds to most things: loudly, creatively, and with significant bass.

This connection between Atlanta's music culture and its basketball team is not accidental. The Hawks have actively collaborated with Atlanta artists, built playlists that reflect the city's taste, and positioned the arena experience as something that feels distinctly local rather than generic. When a Hawks game is clicking and the crowd is fully engaged, the building sounds like it belongs to a city that has always done things its own way.

18. The Dunk Contest and the Hawks' Complicated Relationship With Glory

The NBA Slam Dunk Contest has produced some of the most memorable moments in All-Star Weekend history, and Atlanta has been responsible for a disproportionate share of them. Dominique Wilkins won the contest in 1985 and 1990, delivering performances that players still reference when debating the greatest dunkers of all time. More on his specific flights of athletic genius in Chapters 2 and 3.

Beyond Dominique, the Hawks have sent multiple players to the contest over the decades with varying degrees of success and spectacle. The franchise has a cultural relationship with above-the-rim basketball that goes back decades, partly because of Wilkins and partly because Atlanta has consistently drafted and developed athletes whose most natural form of expression is going directly over whoever is in their way.

Jalen Johnson, the Hawks' current cornerstone, declared his intention to enter the 2026 Slam Dunk Contest during All-Star Weekend media day, keeping the Atlanta tradition very much alive. For a city that treats spectacular athletic moments as a birthright, having a player willing to carry that torch into a new era is less a surprise and more a requirement. Hawks fans expect the dunk contest. They always have.

19. Ted Turner, Time Warner, and the Most Distracted Owner in NBA History

For a significant chunk of Hawks history, the team was owned by a man who also owned a cable news network, a baseball team, a movie studio, and approximately one million other things. Ted Turner acquired the Hawks in 1977 and ran them with the same restless, maximalist energy he applied to everything else in his life, which is to say with enormous enthusiasm and occasional chaos.

Turner was genuinely passionate about the team, which made it all the more interesting when his attention was clearly somewhere else. He once briefly served as the

Atlanta Braves' field manager for a single game, which is the kind of decision that only makes sense when you own the team and also own CNN and also are Turner Broadcasting and also are in the middle of building a global media empire. The Hawks were one item on a very long list.

Time Warner eventually absorbed Turner's empire in 2001, meaning the Hawks were briefly owned by one of the largest media corporations on the planet. This is a bit like your school basketball team being sponsored by a country. The franchise was sold to a private ownership group in 2004, which meant the Hawks could once again be owned by people who only had to think about owning the Hawks. The organizational focus improved noticeably.

20. Nicknames, Chants, and the Language of Being a Hawks Fan

Every fanbase develops its own language over time, a collection of nicknames, chants, and references that separate people who actually follow the team from people who are pretending to. Hawks fans have built up a rich vocabulary over the decades, and using it correctly in a conversation is a reliable way to prove your credentials.

"Nique" required no further explanation in Atlanta for the better part of two decades. "Ice Trae" arrived as a nickname because Trae Young had a habit of performing his best basketball when the pressure was highest, a trait that Atlanta fans appreciated deeply after years of watching opponents fold in big moments. "Spida" Mitchell visited and Hawks fans booed him politely but thoroughly. These things matter in ways that are difficult to explain to people who do not follow basketball closely but are immediately obvious to anyone who does.

The Hawks fanbase has also developed a specific pride around being underestimated, a tradition born from years of being the Eastern Conference's most interesting team that nobody outside Georgia seemed to want to talk about. Atlanta fans have largely decided that this is fine. They know what they have. They have always known what they have. The rest of the world tends to find out eventually.

21. The Trae Young Story: All of It

The trade that brought Trae Young to Atlanta on draft night in 2018 looked like a gamble. The Hawks sent the fifth overall pick to Dallas, which used it to select Luka Doncic, a European teenager who would go on to become one of the best players on the planet. Atlanta took Young with the third pick instead. The internet spent the next several months explaining why this was a catastrophic mistake, which made it considerably more satisfying when it turned out not to be.

Young became a four-time All-Star, the franchise's all-time assists leader, and one of the most entertaining players in the league. He led the Hawks to the Eastern Conference Finals in 2021, silencing arenas full of people who had decided to root against him. For several seasons, he was the most important player in Atlanta sports and the most polarizing point guard in the NBA, depending entirely on which side of his pull-up three-pointer you happened to be standing on.

Then, in January 2026, the Hawks traded him to Washington. Young had asked out, the team had found a new cornerstone in Jalen Johnson, and both sides were ready to move on. It ended not with a dramatic collapse but with a quiet, mutual understanding that the next chapter needed a different main character. The Trae Young era in Atlanta was entertaining, maddening, brilliant, and ultimately incomplete. That combination is not the worst legacy a player can leave. It is, in fact, a very Atlanta kind of story.

22. Jalen Johnson: Atlanta Did Not See This Coming (But Maybe Should Have)

Jalen Johnson was drafted by the Hawks in 2021 and spent his first few seasons doing enough impressive things that people who watched closely kept saying his name while people who watched casually kept forgetting it. Then came the 2025-26 season, and suddenly nobody was forgetting it anymore.

Johnson, a 6-foot-8 forward with the handle of a point guard and the defensive instincts of someone who takes that part of the game personally, averaged a triple-double in the month of December 2025. LeBron James compared his potential to Scottie Pippen, which is not a comparison LeBron makes casually or often. Johnson was named an All-Star for the first time in

February 2026, becoming the undisputed face of the franchise in the same season the previous face of the franchise was traded away. He did not seem rattled by any of it. His response when asked about the pressure of being the new guy in Atlanta was essentially that he had been preparing for this his whole career and was not planning to waste the preparation.

The Hawks built their post-Trae roster around his specific skills: length, playmaking, two-way versatility, and a competitive temperament that makes teammates play better just by proximity. He is the kind of player franchises wait years to find and then spend years trying to keep. Atlanta found him in the draft. That never stops being a good story.

23. The Trades That Built Something Real

The roster around Jalen Johnson did not appear by accident. It was assembled through a series of moves that looked questionable in isolation and increasingly intelligent in combination, which is honestly the best way to build an NBA team if you can pull it off.

Dejounte Murray arrived from San Antonio in 2022, bringing defensive intensity and playmaking to a team that needed both. He was later traded to New Orleans in 2024, and what came back was Dyson Daniels, a 6-foot-8 point-of-attack defender who immediately made Atlanta harder to score against and considerably more annoying to play. Nickeil Alexander-Walker arrived as a free agent and turned into one of the best secondary creators in the East. Zaccharie Risacher, taken with the second overall pick in the 2025 draft, added another long athletic wing to a lineup that was increasingly full of them. The Hawks were quietly building a team that looked less like a collection of individual talents and more like a coordinated defensive organism. Other teams started noticing this around the same time their offensive field goal percentages started dropping.

Every piece came from somewhere different. Every piece fit. That does not happen often, and when it does, the front office deserves the credit that fans eventually remember to give them.

24. Draft Capital and the Art of Playing Chess While Everyone Else Plays Checkers

One of the least glamorous but most important things the Atlanta Hawks have done in recent years is accumulate future draft picks the way some people collect things they will definitely find useful later and currently have no room for. The Hawks entered 2026 holding future first-round selections from the New Orleans Pelicans and Milwaukee Bucks, two franchises that have not made the Hawks' life easy in recent playoff history, which makes holding their draft futures feel like a small but satisfying form of justice.

The Pelicans pick in particular carries significant lottery potential, meaning Atlanta could add another high-upside player to an already interesting young core. Combined with approximately thirty million dollars in projected cap space heading into the offseason, the Hawks are positioned to be one of the more active and flexible teams in the league over the next several years. This is the part of team-building that does not generate highlights or get discussed much on sports radio but tends to determine which franchises are actually good five years from now rather than just appearing to be good right now.

Building a contender in the NBA requires patience, smart drafting, cap discipline, and occasionally trading away a four-time All-Star who asked for a fresh start. The Hawks have done all of these things. The chess is being played. The pieces are on the board.

25. Hawks Tomorrow: The Window Is Open

The Atlanta Hawks enter their next chapter as one of the more intriguing teams in the Eastern Conference, which is a sentence that has been written about Atlanta basketball several times over the past decade with varying degrees of accuracy. The difference this time is that the foundation looks different than it has before.

Jalen Johnson is 24 years old and playing the best basketball of his career. Dyson Daniels is 22. Zaccharie Risacher is 19. The core is not aging toward a window, it is sitting inside one that has several years of useful light left. The team won ten consecutive games after the trade deadline, posted one of the better net ratings in the league during that stretch, and did it with a defensive identity that previous Hawks teams never really had. Atlanta has historically been a team that tried to outscore problems. This version of the Hawks tries to make problems go away before they become points.

The city is paying attention in a way it did not always during the Trae Young years, when the brilliance was real but the winning felt perpetually one piece away. Atlanta is a city that gives its full heart to teams it believes in. The Hawks are giving it reasons to believe. That combination, in a building that already sounds like a music venue when it gets loud, is worth watching.

Bonus Trivia Quiz!

You think you are a true Hawks fan? Try this bonus quiz!

1. The Atlanta Hawks originally played under what name when the franchise launched in 1946?

A) The Atlanta Blackhawks
B) The Tri-Cities Blackhawks
C) The Milwaukee Hawks
D) The St. Louis Blackhawks

2. Which three cities shared the original Tri-Cities franchise?

A) Chicago, Peoria, and Springfield
B) Memphis, Nashville, and Knoxville
C) Moline, Rock Island, and Davenport
D) Madison, Milwaukee, and Green Bay

3. In what year did the Hawks win their only NBA Championship?

A) 1955
B) 1957
C) 1958
D) 1961

4. How many points did Bob Pettit score in the championship-clinching Game 6 against the Celtics?

A) 40
B) 44
C) 47
D) 50

5. Which record did Bob Pettit achieve that no NBA player had reached before him?

A) First player to win three MVP awards
B) First player to score 20,000 career points
C) First player to average 30 points per game for a season
D) First player to make ten All-Star teams

6. How many seasons did Pete Maravich play for the Atlanta Hawks?

A) Two
B) Three
C) Four
D) Six

7. What is Dominique Wilkins's official nickname?

A) The Flying Falcon

B) The Dunking Machine

C) The Human Highlight Film

D) The ATL Assassin

8. How many Slam Dunk Contest titles did Dominique Wilkins win?

A) One

B) Two

C) Three

D) Four

9. How many points did Dominique Wilkins score against the Chicago Bulls on December 10, 1986?

A) 50

B) 53

C) 57

D) 61

10. In the famous 1988 playoff duel, how many points did Dominique Wilkins score against Larry Bird and the Celtics in Game 7?

A) 38

B) 41

C) 44

D) 47

11. What was Dikembe Mutombo's iconic post-block gesture?

A) A chest thump toward the crowd

B) A slow finger wag

C) A double fist pump

D) Pointing at the shot clock

12. How many games did the Hawks win in their record-breaking 2014-15 regular season?

A) 54

B) 57

C) 60

D) 63

13. In the 2021 playoffs, which arena did Trae Young silence with a pull-up three-pointer to close out the first round series?

A) TD Garden

B) Barclays Center

C) Madison Square Garden

D) United Center

14. Which team did the Hawks trade Trae Young to in January 2026?

A) Dallas Mavericks

B) Los Angeles Lakers

C) Washington Wizards

D) Chicago Bulls

15. Who became the Hawks' new franchise cornerstone after the Trae Young trade?

A) Dyson Daniels

B) Zaccharie Risacher

C) Nickeil Alexander-Walker

D) Jalen Johnson

Super Fan Secret Challenge

Only a true Hawks fan will know this.

(No Answer Provided)

Before being drafted by the Tri-Cities Blackhawks, the franchise's very first head coach in 1946 also held what other role with the team?

A) Team physician
B) General manager and head coach simultaneously
C) Team owner
D) Radio broadcaster

Answer Key

1. B) The Tri-Cities Blackhawks

2. C) Moline, Rock Island, and Davenport

3. C) 1958

4. D) 50

5. B) First player to score 20,000 career points

6. C) Four

7. C) The Human Highlight Film

8. B) Two

9. C) 57

10. D) 47

11. B) A slow finger wag

12. C) 60

13. C) Madison Square Garden

14. C) Washington Wizards

15. D) Jalen Johnson

NBA PLAYOFF BRACKET

* Fill in your picks and try not to argue with your friends about it!

Part of the Fun Fan Facts: The Unofficial Sports Guide Series

Be the Boss of the Playoffs

You've broken down the matchups. You know which superstar takes over in the fourth quarter. You've seen the bench units that quietly decide series. You've watched the adjustments coaches make when their backs are against the wall.

Now it's time to stop watching and start deciding.

On this page, you are not just a fan. You are the Head Coach drawing up the last play with three seconds left on the clock. You are the GM who built this roster. You are the analyst who saw it all coming.

This is not just filling out a bracket.

This is building your championship run.

Sixteen teams enter the NBA Playoffs. The path is brutal. Best of seven. No shortcuts. No hiding. Every round gets louder, harder, and more personal.

This bracket is your Playoff Control Room.

The Game Plan

1. Survive Round One: Start with the opening round. Which matchup is going seven games? Who has the closer? Who folds under pressure? Make the calls.

2. Feel the Momentum: As you move into the Conference Semifinals and Conference Finals, things change. Role players become heroes. Stars feel the weight. Trust your reads.

3. Own the Finals: Trace your picks all the way to the NBA Finals. When the confetti falls and the trophy is raised, you'll find out who earned it.

House Rules: Circle your boldest upset. That is your official "I knew it" moment.

Choose Your Weapon: Pencil if you want flexibility. Pen if you trust your instincts. Sharpie if you believe in chaos.

Because once the playoffs tip off, there is no rewinding Game 7.

Make your picks. Trust your basketball brain. And let the playoff drama begin.

Fun Facts Wrap-Up

You made it through! You're officially a true superfan! Now it's time to put your knowledge to the test. Share these facts with friends and see who really knows their team best.

Love the series?

Your reviews help other fans discover Fun Fan Facts. If you enjoyed this book, we'd really appreciate you sharing your thoughts and leaving a review.

Want more Fun Fan Facts?

Scan the QR code below to visit our site and explore bonus trivia, challenges, and special extras - including new teams, future series, and collectible fun as they're released.

Collect All the Fun Fan Facts Series!

Check off every book you read. See the full set on Amazon. Search "Fun Fan Facts Jake Liam."

World Cup 2026 Edition

- ☐ Algeria
- ☐ France
- ☐ Paraguay
- ☐ Argentina
- ☐ Germany
- ☐ Portugal
- ☐ Australia
- ☐ Ghana
- ☐ Qatar
- ☐ Austria
- ☐ Haiti
- ☐ Saudi Arabia
- ☐ Belgium
- ☐ Iran
- ☐ Scotland
- ☐ Brazil
- ☐ Ivory Coast
- ☐ Senegal
- ☐ Canada
- ☐ Japan
- ☐ South Africa
- ☐ Cape Verde
- ☐ Jordan
- ☐ South Korea
- ☐ Colombia
- ☐ Mexico
- ☐ Spain
- ☐ Croatia
- ☐ Morocco
- ☐ Switzerland
- ☐ Curaçao
- ☐ Netherlands
- ☐ Tunisia
- ☐ Ecuador
- ☐ New Zealand
- ☐ United States
- ☐ Egypt
- ☐ Norway
- ☐ Uruguay
- ☐ England
- ☐ Panama
- ☐ Uzbekistan

World Cup 2026 Group Edition

- ☐ Group A
- ☐ Group E
- ☐ Group I
- ☐ Group B
- ☐ Group F
- ☐ Group J
- ☐ Group C
- ☐ Group G
- ☐ Group K
- ☐ Group D
- ☐ Group H
- ☐ Group L

English Football Edition

☐ Arsenal F.C.   ☐ Manchester City

☐ Aston Villa F.C.   ☐ Manchester United

☐ Chelsea F.C.   ☐ Newcastle United F.C.

☐ Everton F.C.   ☐ Tottenham Hotspur

☐ Fulham F.C.   ☐ West Ham United

☐ Liverpool F.C.   ☐ Wrexham A.F.C.

NBA Edition

☐ Atlanta Hawks   ☐ Miami Heat

☐ Boston Celtics   ☐ Milwaukee Bucks

☐ Brooklyn Nets   ☐ Minnesota Timberwolves

☐ Charlotte Hornets   ☐ New Orleans Pelicans

☐ Chicago Bulls   ☐ New York Knicks

☐ Cleveland Cavaliers   ☐ Oklahoma City Thunder

☐ Dallas Mavericks   ☐ Orlando Magic

☐ Denver Nuggets   ☐ Philadelphia 76ers

☐ Detroit Pistons   ☐ Phoenix Suns

☐ Golden State Warriors   ☐ Portland Trail Blazers

☐ Houston Rockets   ☐ Sacramento Kings

☐ Indiana Pacers   ☐ San Antonio Spurs

☐ LA Clippers   ☐ Toronto Raptors

☐ Los Angeles Lakers   ☐ Utah Jazz

☐ Memphis Grizzlies   ☐ Washington Wizards

About the Author

Jake is a 13-year-old sports fan who loves football, American football, and basketball. He plays soccer as a goalie and dreams of one day playing for West Ham United and helping teach kids to love the game. His passion for sports runs in the family - his dad was a professional baseball player, and his stepdad sparked his love for West Ham. Through the Fun Fan Facts series, he shares the fun and excitement of sports with fans everywhere.

9 781972 300107